THE EYE AND SEEING

Revised Edition
Steve Parker

Series Consultant
Dr Alan Maryon-Davis
MB, BChir, MSc, MRCP, FFCM

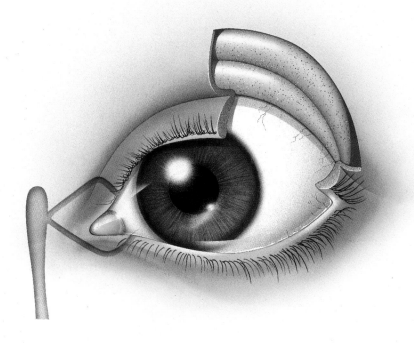

Franklin Watts
London • New York • Toronto • Sydney

Words marked in bold appear in the glossary.

© **1989 Franklin Watts**
Original edition first published in 1982

Published in the United States by
Franklin Watts Inc.
387 Park Avenue South
New York, NY 10016

ISBN: 0 531 10654 3
Library of Congress Catalog Card Number: 88 51606

Illustrations: Andrew Aloof, Marion Appleton, Nick Cudworth,
Howard Dyke, David Holmes, David Mallott and Angela Owen. By
courtesy of the British Museum (Natural History).

Photographs: Chris Fairclough 29, 31, 34. Science Photo Library:
Martin Dohrn 5, 11; Ralph Eagle 13; Petit Format/E M de
Monasterio 20; David Parker 21, 35; Robin Scagell 43. Sony UK
Limited 43. ZEFA Cover, 33, 37.

Printed in Belgium

Contents

The sense of sight

The human body has six main senses – seeing, hearing, smell, balance, and taste. But our sense of sight dominates our lives. Four-fifths of all the information received by the brain comes in through our eyes. Our eyes are so important that they tend to overwhelm our other senses. We often close our eyes when we want to concentrate on hearing – when we listen to a piece of music, for example.

Compared to most other animals, humans have good vision. Some animals can only see vague patches of light and dark. We can see clearly in daylight and reasonably well in the dark. We can also judge the distance of an object. And we can see in color.

Our eyes see an area, called the **field of vision**, which stretches from one shoulder to the other and from the forehead down to the waist. By turning the head, we can see above, below and behind us. But our eyes are only part of the process of seeing. The other part involves the brain.

It is in the brain, in our "mind's eye," that we put together and make sense of our pictures of the world. Scientists understand much about how the eye itself works. But they still do not know the full details of how we see, especially how we learn to recognize patterns, shapes and movements. Computers have trouble "seeing" as well as a child of three. Even with an advanced program, a computer finds it hard to tell the difference between a tree and a telegraph pole!

Types of eyes

In the animal kingdom, there are many different types of eyes, each adapted to the conditions in which the particular creature lives.

- Simple eyes, as found in animals such as worms, can react to light changes but do not form images.
- Compound eyes are those in which hundreds or thousands of light-sensitive units are joined together, as in many insects.

- Cat's eyes have an extra layer or membrane behind the retina, which reflects light back onto the retina. This makes cat's eyes look as if they glow in the dark.
- Some creatures, such as snakes, have an extra eyelid which slides across the eye to give added protection.
- Some fish have eyes split into two parts so that when they swim close to the surface, one part of each eye sees in air while the other sees in water.

△ The human eye is a very complex and fragile organ. A healthy human eye can see well in dim or bright light. It can also detect different colors and see near and distant objects clearly.

The marvelous eyeball

The "eyeball" is well named. The human eye is indeed shaped like a ball. It measures 2.5 cm (1 in) across and weighs around 7 g (0.25 oz).

The outer layer of the eyeball, the **sclera**, is made of tough, white, fibrous tissue. This is what we call the "white" of the eye. At the front of the eye, in the middle, the sclera becomes transparent and allows light to pass through. This area is called the **cornea.**

The cornea is covered by a delicate membrane, the **conjunctiva**, which is also transparent. The conjunctiva produces fluid and, together with the tear glands, keeps the front of the eye clean and moist.

Inside the sclera is a thin, dark red layer called the **choroid**. This contains blood vessels, which nourish the various layers of the eye. It also contains pigmented cells that absorb light and prevent it from being reflected back on to the light-sensitive layer of the eye. At the front of the eye, the choroid layer becomes the muscular **iris**. In the center of the iris is a hole, called the **pupil**, through which light passes into the eye.

Inside the choroid is another layer, the **retina**. The retina contains the cells that detect light and turn it into electrical nerve messages. The messages are carried by nerves that pass through the back of the eye to the optic nerve, which goes to the brain. Where all the nerves leave the eye, there is no room for light-sensitive retinal cells. This area cannot detect light, so it is called the **blind spot**.

▽ The yellow circle on this diagram shows the blind spot on the retina. Here there are no light-sensitive cells.

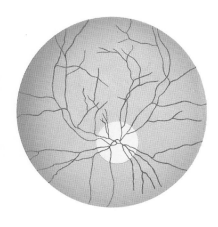

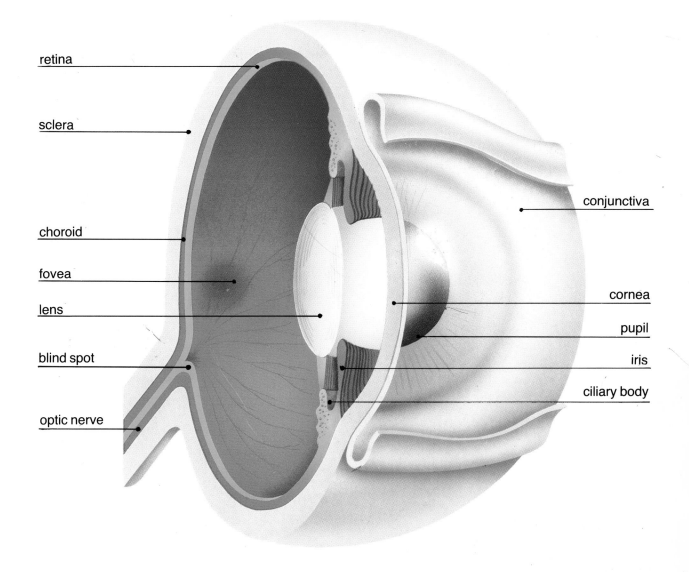

retina

sclera

choroid

fovea

lens

blind spot

optic nerve

conjunctiva

cornea

pupil

iris

ciliary body

The eyeball is divided into two chambers. The front chamber, behind the cornea, contains a clear liquid, the **aqueous humor**. At the back of this chamber lies the iris and behind the iris is the **lens**. The lens is transparent and focuses light onto the retina. The chamber behind the lens, which makes up the bulk of the eyeball, contains a clear jelly called **vitreous humor**.

△ This section through the human eye shows all the main structures involved in seeing. Light enters the eye through the pupil. It passes through the lens, and an image falls on the retina. This information is passed to the brain along the **optic nerve**.

The eye – the first camera

The eye is like a camera – or rather the camera is like an eye, since eyes have been around for several hundred million years longer than cameras. Both the camera and the eye have light-proof, protective cases and a small transparent "window" through which light enters. The amount of light coming in must be controlled to prevent over-exposure and damage in very bright light and to admit as much light as possible in very dim conditions. In the eye, this job is done by the iris, which becomes wider or narrower and so changes the size of the pupil (the "window"). The camera has a similar mechanism, a circular shutter that changes the size of the aperture or "window."

▷ Light enters a camera through the lens. The lens focuses the image upside down on the film at the back of the camera.

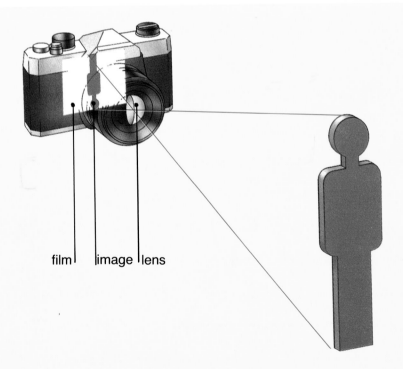

film   image   lens

Without a focusing mechanism, both the eye and a camera would just see a huge, multi-colored blur. A lens carries out the fine focusing of light rays and forms a clear, sharp image – on the retina of the eye and on the film in a camera. The two focusing mechanisms are, however, slightly different. In the eye, the lens itself changes shape to focus the light. In a camera, the lens moves backward and forward for focusing.

In a camera, the image is recorded on light-sensitive chemicals in the film. The eye also uses light-sensitive chemicals in the cells of the retina but the chemicals transform light into electrical messages, which are sent to the brain.

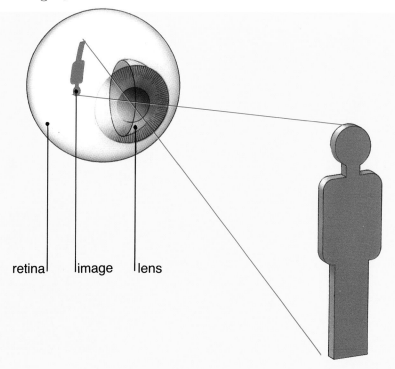

retina | image | lens

◁ Light enters the human eye through the cornea. It passes through the pupil and lens and the image is focused upside down on the retina.

Letting in light

When we talk about the color of someone's eyes, we are referring to the iris, with its black hole (the pupil) in the middle. The iris is named after the Greek word for "rainbow," and it contains pigment cells which give the various eye colors. The colors and patterns on the iris are thought to be unique to each person, like fingerprints. The color of our eyes has nothing to do with how well they see.

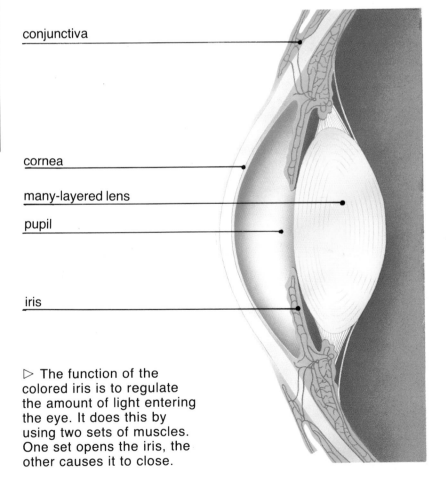

conjunctiva

cornea

many-layered lens

pupil

iris

▷ The function of the colored iris is to regulate the amount of light entering the eye. It does this by using two sets of muscles. One set opens the iris, the other causes it to close.

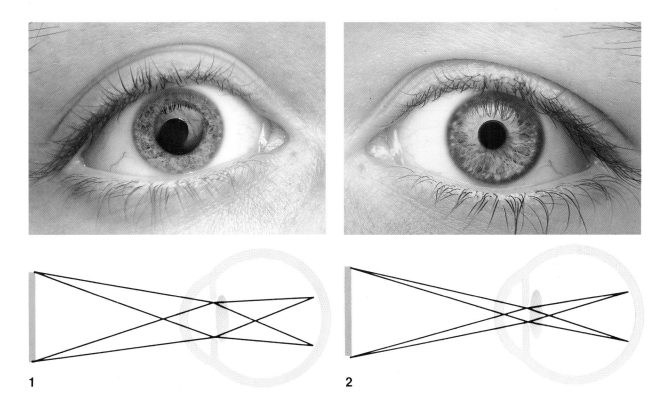

1   **2**

As light conditions change, muscles within the iris lengthen or shorten to change the size of the pupil and control the amount of light entering the eye. In dim light, the pupil may widen to 8 mm (0.3 in) across, allowing more light to reach the retina. In bright light, the pupil can be as small as a pin-prick.

The iris changes shape automatically. When very bright light enters the eye, it is detected by the retina, and almost at once its pupil contracts. This is a reflex safety reaction which does not involve the brain directly – the brain may be busy dealing with other matters and so could delay things slightly.

The pupil of the human eye is round, as in many other daytime animals. Pupils of other creatures come in a variety of shapes. The pupils of a cat are vertical slits which can open very wide for night-time prowling.

△ The size of the pupil is controlled by the iris.
1 When light is weak, the muscles of the iris open up, or dilate, making the pupil larger to allow more light to enter the eye.
2 When light is strong the iris contracts, making the pupil smaller. In these diagrams, and in all others in this book, light rays are shown as straight lines.

Focusing the lens

Light rays entering the eye must be focused or "bent" so that they form a clear, sharp image on the retina. Most of this bending is done by a combination of the curved cornea, the anterior tear film layer and the lens (much as light rays are bent when you look into a swimming pool). About one-quarter of the focusing power, and the fine adjustments to focusing the light rays, are carried out by the lens.

▽ The lens is suspended between the cornea and the retina by ligaments. These, in turn, are joined to the ciliary muscles.

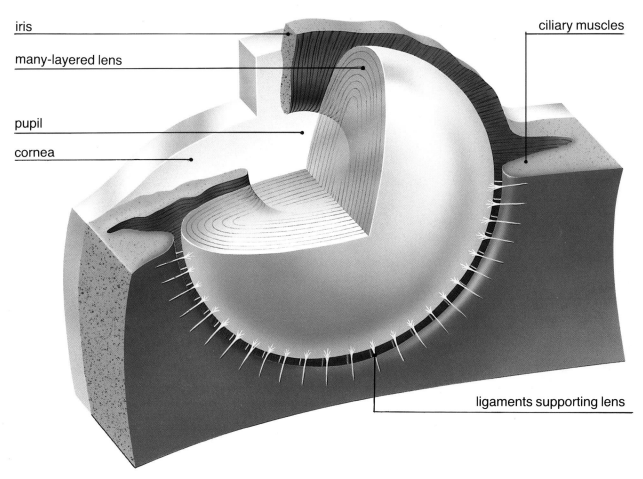

iris

many-layered lens

pupil

cornea

ciliary muscles

ligaments supporting lens

The lens is about the size of a pea and lies just behind the iris. It is very clear, although slightly yellow, and is made of layers of cells, like the layers of an onion. The shape of the lens is biconvex — that is, it is thicker in the middle than around the edges. It is also slightly flatter at the front than at the back.

Around the lens is a transparent, elastic capsule. The lens in its capsule resembles a clear plastic bag filled with a faintly yellow jelly. The capsule is suspended from the **ciliary muscles** around the lens by strong, thread-like ligaments. It is rather like a circular trampoline suspended in its frame by elastic straps. The ciliary muscles are, in turn, attached to the sclera, the tough white covering of the eye.

To bring distant objects into focus, the ciliary muscles relax and the sclera (which is stretched by the pressure of the vitreous humor) pulls the lens into a thin, flat shape. To allow us to focus on nearby objects, the ciliary muscles contract and shorten. This releases the lens from the pull of the sclera so the lens bulges outward. The ciliary muscles must work to allow us to see near objects clearly and relax to allow us to focus on distant objects.

Sometimes the lens goes cloudy, a condition called **cataract**. The person cannot see clearly and may need an operation. One type of operation removes the lens completely; the patient is then given special eyeglasses to wear. The eye is no longer able to see both distant and near objects clearly, but imperfect sight is better than not being able to see at all. A different type of operation involves removing the lens substance from inside the capsule and replacing it with a clear, jelly-like artificial substitute. By this means, the lens can still focus on objects.

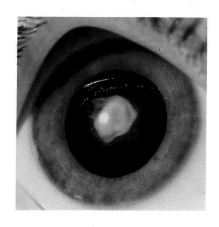

△ A condition called **cataract** makes the lens cloudy, sometimes causing loss of vision. Cataracts are most commonly found in old people, but they can also be caused by infections (even in newborn babies), or by the effects of other diseases, such as diabetes.

Focus and accommodation

If our eyes did not have lenses inside them to focus the light and allow us to see things clearly, the world would look very different. Animals without lenses in their eyes probably see their surroundings only as a blurred mosaic of light and dark patches.

As light rays pass through the eye, they are bent toward each other and eventually cross. For us to see a clear, focused image, this cross-over point must fall exactly on the retina. If the point where the light rays cross falls in front of, or behind, the retina, we see a blurred, out-of-focus image. We say we are far- or nearsighted.

Light rays from distant objects arrive at the eye almost parallel to each other and need less bending. Light rays from near objects diverge from each other and must be bent more sharply. The lens in the eye is rubbery and flexible and its shape can be changed in order to focus on close or distant images. The shape can be changed almost instantly and is under the control of the brain.

When we look from a distant to a close object, the image is blurred for a fraction of a second because it takes time for the ciliary muscles to contract and allow the lens to bulge to its fat, powerful shape. This is called **accommodation**. Normally it is so rapid that we rarely notice it. When we look back to a distant object, the ciliary muscles relax and the sclera pulls the lens into its flat, less powerful shape. If you are doing close work or reading, it is a good idea to look into the distance from time to time in order to rest the eyes.

▽ How the lens changes shape.
1 When the ciliary muscles around the lens contract, they release the tension on the ligaments holding the lens in shape and the lens bulges into a more rounded shape.
2 When the ciliary muscles relax, the tension on the ligaments pulls the lens into a more flattened shape.

1   2

A newborn baby cannot focus on objects far away. The focusing mechanism in its eyes is fixed on objects about 20–30 cm (8–12 in) away. This is about the distance between the baby's face and its mother's face when she is feeding it. The eye is best at accommodation during the early teens. It loses the ability with age, as the lens becomes less elastic.

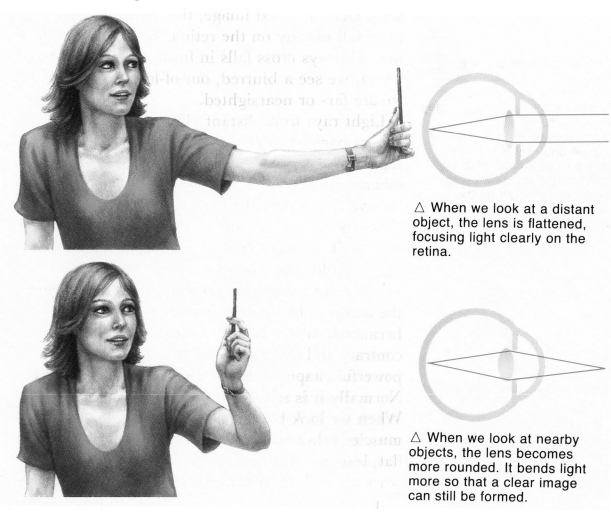

△ When we look at a distant object, the lens is flattened, focusing light clearly on the retina.

△ When we look at nearby objects, the lens becomes more rounded. It bends light more so that a clear image can still be formed.

15

Seeing in 3-D

Close one eye and look ahead. Then open it and close the other eye. You will find that the view changes slightly and objects in the foreground, such as a window frame, seem to jump across things in the background. The eyes are about 6 cm (2.5 in) apart so each eye sees a slightly different picture of the world. The brain compares these pictures in order to judge how far away things are. It does this partly from experience and partly by measuring the angles at which the eyes are turned inward.

When you look at something, the eyes angle themselves so that the important part of the image falls on a particularly sensitive part of the retina, the **fovea**. Here the greatest detail is seen. To look at a distant object, each eye points straight ahead so the image falls on the fovea. The picture seen by each eye is almost the same. But to look at a nearby object, the eyes turn inward much more and their views of the object are more different. The brain detects the degree to which they turn inward, which is called **convergence**. The greater the convergence, the nearer the object must be.

When an object is too close to see clearly, you go "cross-eyed." Children, whose eyes are closer together, can view things clearly as close as 7.5 cm (3 in). For most adults, objects closer than about 15 cm (6 in) become blurred. With your finger about 30 cm (12 in) away, gradually bring it closer to your eyes while watching it carefully. When it comes too close you see two fingers, one in each eye.

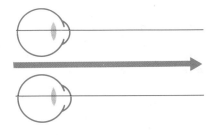

△ The eyes look in the same direction when viewing a distant object.

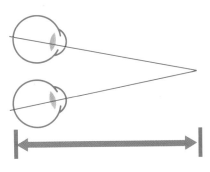

△ To view something very close, both eyes look slightly inward so that light still falls on the most sensitive area of the retina.

16

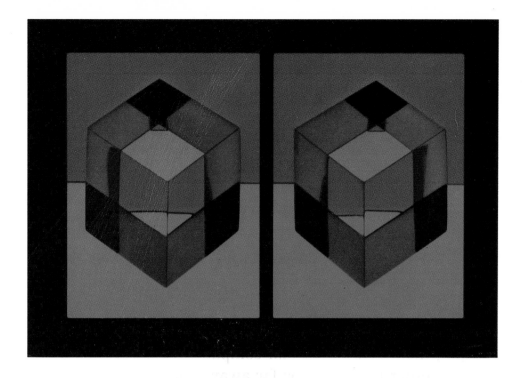

The ability to judge distance using two eyes side by side is called **stereoscopic**, binocular or three-dimensional (3-D) vision. It gives depth to what we see and makes it easy for us to reach out, touch and manipulate things. Humans do not have the best stereoscopic vision in the animal kingdom, but it is still fairly good. It has probably contributed to the success of our species – for example in helping us to use tools.

Stereoscopic vision is, however, only one aspect of the way in which we judge distance. Several other aspects are learned by the brain as general rules. One is **perspective**. This causes an object, such as a car, to look big when it is near and small when it is farther away. Another clue is **parallax**: when we move the head from side to side, nearer things appear to move across in front of distant ones. Sports people who are aiming at a target sometimes shift their position to help them judge the distance of the target. Other clues used by the brain include the haze in front of faraway objects and the dimming of colors with distance.

△ Take a piece of cardboard, the size of an envelope, and place it on the line between these two stereoscopic pictures. Bring your face very close to the edge of the cardboard so that your left eye sees only the left-hand picture and the right eye sees only the right-hand picture. The scene should appear in 3-D.

17

The retina

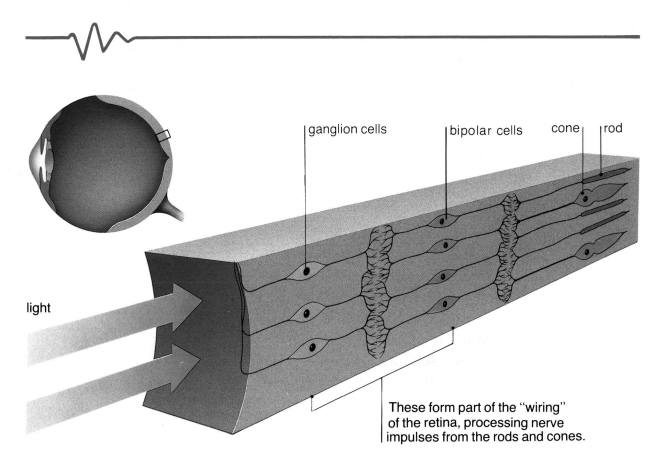

ganglion cells   bipolar cells   cone   rod

light

These form part of the "wiring" of the retina, processing nerve impulses from the rods and cones.

△ The retina is made up of several layers of cells. It can process and alter images falling on its surface before they are passed on to the brain. The light-sensitive rods and cones are at the **back** of the retina.

The retina is one of the most astonishing parts of the body. It is a transparent sheet of tissue, shaped like a deep cup, which is only $\frac{1}{10}$ mm ($\frac{1}{250}$th in) thick and about the size of a postage stamp. Yet it can detect a detailed, continuous and moving view of the world in color. The retina converts light rays into electrical messages (nerve impulses) and sends these impulses along the optic nerve to the brain.

The retina itself is made of several layers. The outermost layer has more than 130 million light-sensitive cells called **rods** and **cones**. When light falls on a rod or a cone, the cell sends nerve impulses to a network of nerve cells called **bipolar cells**. These cells are in turn connected to another

◁ Close your left eye and stare at the round spot on the left. Move the page gradually closer to your eye, and when it is about 20 cm (8 in) away, the cross will vanish. Its image is now falling on the blind spot on your retina.

layer of cells, called **ganglion cells**. Each of these layers is inside the retina, which means that light must pass through them in order to reach the rods and cones. This is not a particularly efficient design. However the brain soon learns to cope with these "shadows" thrown into the retina by the nerve cells and also blood vessels.

Scientists are only just beginning to understand how these layers work. The rods, cones, bipolar cells, ganglion cells and other types of cells are interconnected so that they pass messages to the optic nerve only if they "see" a certain type of image. Some groups of cells are very sensitive to spots; others react to lines. Some cells respond to movement in one direction, while others respond to movement in a different direction. All this happens almost instantly.

The result is that the messages leaving the retina along the optic nerve are already highly sorted, processed and coded. In fact there are only about 800,000 nerve fibers leaving the eye, so the millions of impulses from the rods and cones have been modified by more than 99 percent.

The retina also contains blood vessels that nourish it. The nerves and blood vessels leave the eye at the back. Here there are no light-sensitive cells, and this point is known as the **blind spot**.

Even though the image on the retina is upside down and back to front (just as in a camera), the brain quickly learns to turn the image the right way up and exchange left for right.

Looking into your own eye

Normally the brain ignores what it sees of the retina and the blood vessels that cover it, but it is possible to "see" the image of these blood vessels, using a penlight (which should be dim, not powerful).

Close your eye and gently hold the penlight against your upper eyelid. Move the light in very small regular circles and an image will appear, looking like a gnarled tree. This image is of the blood vessels on your retina. When you stop moving the light, the image fades. By moving the light, you have drawn the brain's attention to what it thinks is a moving object. When the image stops moving, the brain ignores it.

Rods and cones

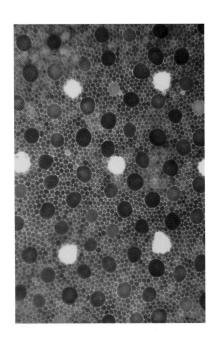

The light-sensitive rod and cone cells in the retina are named for the shape of their top segments. Rods work well in dim light and "see" in shades of gray. Cones work only in bright light but react quickly and "see" in great detail and in color.

In each eye, there are about 125 million rods, which are spread over most of the retina. Rods are about 100 times more sensitive to light than cones. Each rod cell contains millions of molecules of a light-sensitive chemical called **rhodopsin** (or visual purple). When light strikes a molecule of rhodopsin,

△ This microscope photograph shows the rod and cone cells in the human retina. The cones are the larger yellow and dark-green circles, while the rods are the small green shapes that make a honeycomb-like pattern. In this part of the retina, rods outnumber cones by about 20 to 1.

▷ Light stimulates the rods and cones to produce a nerve impulse. At the same time, the rhodopsin in the rods is bleached white. As differing amounts of light fall on different parts of the retina, so the light-sensitive cells being stimulated will vary.

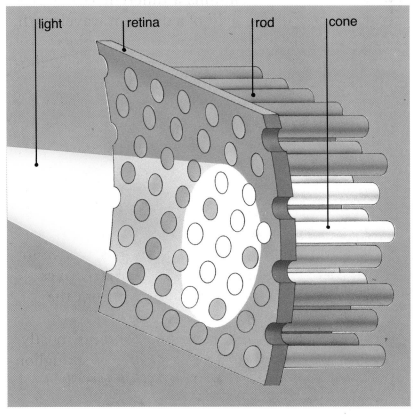

light   retina   rod   cone

it generates a tiny electrical signal. Signals are "pooled" until there are enough to trigger off a message to the nerve cells of the retina.

During the day, visual purple is gradually used up. It is replaced at night but Vitamin A is needed for this process. A shortage of Vitamin A in a person's diet can lead to poor vision in dim light (night blindness).

There are about seven million cones in each eye. Cones are shorter and thicker than rods and react to light four times faster. There are three types of cone, each of which contains a different visual pigment that responds to light of a different wavelength. One responds to long wavelengths (red colors), a second to medium (yellow-green colors) and a third to short wavelengths (blue-violet colors).

Near the center of the back of the retina is the very sensitive area called the fovea or **yellow spot**. It is about 1 mm (1/25th in) across. Here there are no rods, and the cones are narrower than usual and packed more tightly together. Each ganglion cell is connected to only a few cone cells. When you look straight at an object, its image falls on the fovea where vision is precise, finely detailed, sensitive to fast movement, and in color. The brain receives more information from the fovea than from the whole of the rest of the retina.

Away from the fovea, the retina contains mostly rod cells, with up to 300 connected to one ganglion cell. Vision from this area is less precise and in black and white and shades of gray.

Infrared

The human eye cannot see infrared rays. They are given off by objects in relation to their temperature. Special cameras and films are sensitive to infrared and can produce an accurate picture of anything that is sending out infrared rays. Infrared techniques are often used for detecting diseases such as tumors and for finding people who are buried in avalanches or earthquakes.

△ This picture of a palm tree has been taken using film that is sensitive to infrared rays. The green vegetation appears in red here because it is giving out more heat than the bark of the tree.

Looking and seeing

Tunnel vision

Glaucoma is a condition in which there is a build-up of aqueous humor in the eye. This leads to increased pressure on the optic nerve. One of the results of glaucoma is tunnel vision. The nerve fibers dealing with peripheral vision die, and so sufferers are unable to see the things to the side of them. Glaucoma may be treated by drugs or by surgery if it is discovered at an early stage.

The whole area we can see with both eyes is called the visual field. Each eye sees a roughly circular picture of the world. But these pictures are not quite the same because each eye looks at the surroundings from a slightly different angle. Where the two pictures overlap, the brain compares the differences between them as part of its depth judgement for **stereoscopic vision**. Vision is very clear in this area of overlap because there is twice as much information reaching the brain. What one eye misses, the other eye may detect. The visual field of the two eyes together is roughly eyeglass-shaped, with each side of a lower central wedge (obscured by the nose) seen by only one eye.

In each eye, there are separate visual fields for the various types of light-sensitive cells (rods and cones) in the retina because these cells are arranged differently over the retina. The visual field of the rods is the largest, although it is faint in the middle because there are few rods in the center of the retina. The visual field of the green cones is the smallest because these cells are packed closely together in the center of the retina. Although each cone responds mainly to one of the three colors, it also has a few molecules of the other two visual pigments. So there is some overlap and blending of the colors we see.

Color vision is accurate only when we look directly at an object and the image falls on the fovea. Rods, spread around the rest of the retina, see mainly movement and less distinct, colorless

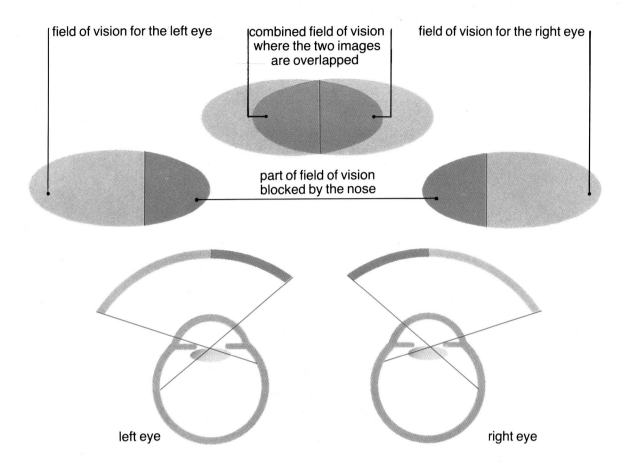

field of vision for the left eye

combined field of vision where the two images are overlapped

field of vision for the right eye

part of field of vision blocked by the nose

left eye

right eye

shapes. This is called **peripheral vision**. A sudden movement detected by the rods on the edge of our vision may cause the eyes to swivel so that the image falls on the fovea and we can examine it in more detail.

When we stare hard at something, it may seem as if our eyes do not move at all. But research has shown that the eyes continually dart quickly around the central part of a scene in a zig-zag fashion, so that the image of each part in turn falls on the fovea for an instant. If we look at a human face, for example, our gaze jumps about to examine each part of the face, especially the eyes, several times. If we watch a person talking, our gaze tends to concentrate on the mouth instead.

△ The picture we see is a combination of the two different images received by the two eyes. These overlap and are adjusted in the brain to produce an accurate picture.

From the eye to the brain

At the back of the brain, in the **visual cortex**, information from the eyes is sifted, coordinated and interpreted.

The optic nerve from each eye does not run separately to the visual cortex. First the optic nerves come together in a central part of the brain, the **optic chiasma**. Here, nerve fibers carrying the left-hand side of each eye's image are split from those carrying the right-hand side of the image. Then the nerves carrying information from the left-hand sides of both eyes come together and continue rearward to the left side of the visual cortex. Similarly, messages from the right-hand sides of each eye are taken to the right side of the visual cortex at the back of the brain.

It is still far from clear how the visual cortex sorts out information from the eyes. Research has shown that some nerve cells in the visual cortex respond to the angles of lines while others are activated by a moving image. Piece by piece, the overall picture is built up. It is compared to previous messages, which help to give it recognition

▷ Most of the brain's activity takes place in its wrinkled surface layer, the **cortex**. There is a special area of the cortex for each of the body's senses. The area concerned with sight, the **visual cortex**, is at the back of the brain. Here nerve impulses from the eyes are sorted out to form a picture.

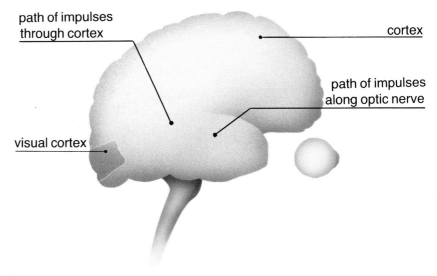

path of impulses through cortex

cortex

path of impulses along optic nerve

visual cortex

24

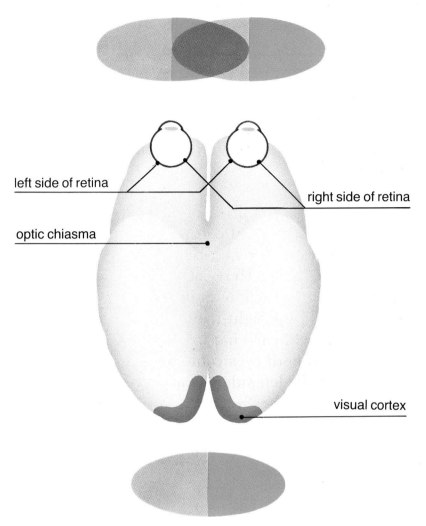

left side of retina

right side of retina

optic chiasma

visual cortex

◁ Light coming from the *right* side of us strikes the *left* side of the retina. It produces nerve impulses that are conveyed to the left side of the brain, to the visual cortex. Light coming from the *left* travels to the *right* side of the visual cortex. The impulses cross each other in the brain and remain.

and meaning. Visual memories are recalled and compared with the present image, as a kind of "short-cut" to identification.

Recognition of some patterns seems to be built into the brain. For instance, newborn babies respond very early to certain important patterns, such as a basic face shape. This putting together of the image involves complex patterns of electrical messages being passed among millions of nerve cells in the visual cortex. Yet it all happens in a fraction of a second.

Eye movement

The eye swivels smoothly in its socket, like a ball in a ballbearing. It is cushioned by pads of fat and its movements are lubricated by special body fluids. Its motion is limited, however, by the short, thick optic nerve. This is fixed to the back of the eyeball and passes through a hole in the bone of the socket on its way to the brain. The socket, or **orbit**, is not round, but somewhat cone-shaped. Wads of fat fill the pointed region at the back, cushioning the optic nerve as it tilts and stretches with each movement of the eye.

Six muscles move the eye with great precision. Each muscle is attached to the socket at one end and the sclera (outermost layer of eyeball) at the other. Most of the muscles are a simple strap shape, but the muscle that pulls the top of the eyeball toward the nose is different. It passes from the back of the socket through a loop called the trochlea, like a cable around a pulley, before it wraps around the eyeball and joins the sclera.

The brain controls eye movements, swiveling both eyes together to keep them aimed at the same thing. Watching a speeding object, such as a racing car, requires split-second monitoring of the position of the image on the retina. As the image moves across the retina, the brain instructs the eye muscles to re-aim the eye constantly, in order to keep the image on the fovea. The neck muscles also take part, turning the head so the eyes can follow the car.

The muscles of the eye

There are six muscles that control the movement of the eye:

- **Superior rectus** moves the eye upward
- **Superior oblique** moves the eye downward and outward
- **Inferior oblique** moves the eye upward and outward
- **Inferior rectus** moves the eye downward
- **Lateral rectus** moves the eye outward
- **Medial rectus** moves the eye inward

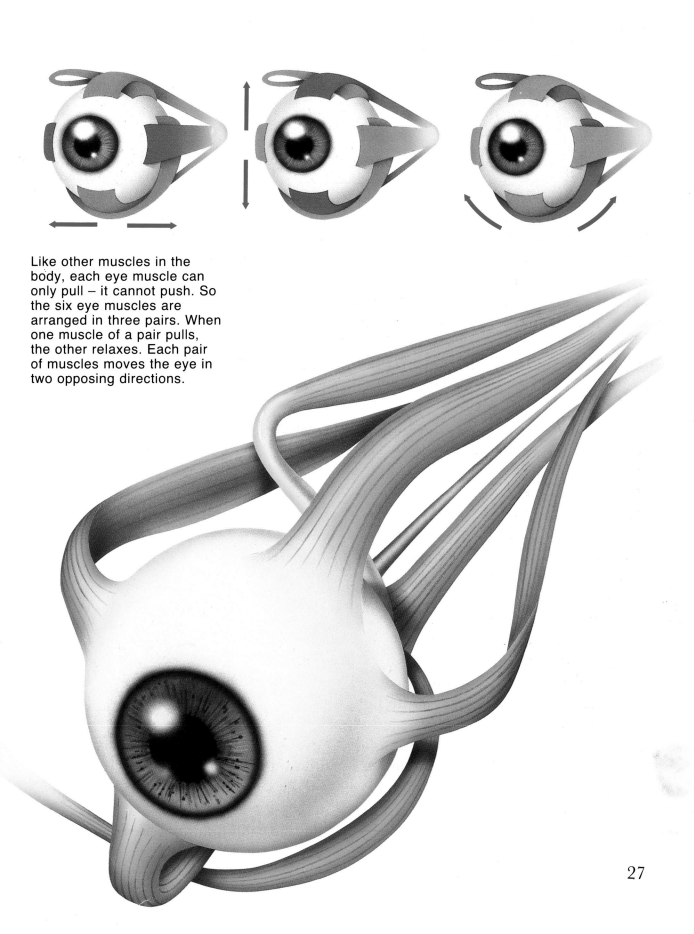

Like other muscles in the body, each eye muscle can only pull – it cannot push. So the six eye muscles are arranged in three pairs. When one muscle of a pair pulls, the other relaxes. Each pair of muscles moves the eye in two opposing directions.

The eye in constant motion

Look carefully at the eyes of someone who is staring steadily at an object. You may be able to see that their eyes are continually moving. This is because the eye muscles shorten by minute amounts every second to give the eye a built-in tremble or "tremor."

If the eye stayed completely still, strong light from bright parts of a scene would fall on the same patch of light-sensitive cells in the retina for some time. The bright light would gradually "bleach" the visual pigments in these cells so they would stop responding to light. But when the eye moves, the bright light falls on a different area of cells. This gives the other cells time to recover and regenerate some of their visual pigments. This "sharing out" of

▽ Our eyes and reading.
1 When we read normally, the eyes scan from side to side along each line as they read the page.
2 Rapid or speed reading uses peripheral vision to take in a whole line at a time, allowing the eyes to move quickly down the page.

1   **2**

the light and dark parts of the scene keeps most of the retinal cells working most of the time.

The restlessness of the eye has another advantage too. If the eye did stay completely still, we would "see" the blind spot, where there are no light-sensitive cells, as a "black hole." The tiny eye movements keep the blind spot moving so that surrounding cells detect missing parts of the picture. These cells send information to the brain, which automatically fills the gap.

Sometimes, however, the restless eye cannot cope. In very bright snow, for example, no areas of retinal cells can be rested. Their visual pigments are soon bleached and after a time, the person cannot see and becomes "snow-blind."

Strabismus

Sometimes there is an imbalance in the strength of the muscles that move the eye. This causes the eye to turn inward (convergent strabismus or cross-eye) or outward (divergent strabismus or wall-eye). The brain blocks out the image received from the affected eye leading to the loss of a whole area of vision. Strabismus, which is also called "squint," may be treated by wearing an eye patch or special eyeglasses, or by surgery.

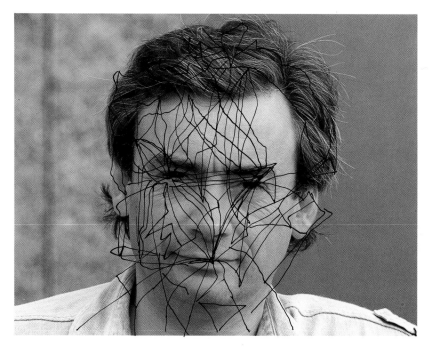

◁ When we look at a person's face, we do not stare straight at him and take in the whole picture at once. These lines show how the viewer's eye roves about, looking at different parts of the face in turn, over a period of about two minutes. We tend to concentrate on the features from which we get most information, mainly around the eyes and mouth. Their expressions give clues as to the person's mood.

29

The blink reflex

The eyes are so important and so delicate they are well protected in several ways. Every few seconds you blink and cannot see. A blink lasts only about one-third of a second but over a whole day this means that you spend about half an hour in the dark. If something comes too close to the eyes, the eyelids close automatically in the **blink reflex**.

The blink washes a watery liquid, called **tear fluid**, over the delicate conjunctiva and cornea. This keeps the surface of the eye from drying out and washes it clean of tiny dust fragments. The fluid is made in the tear gland or **lachrymal gland**, which is roughly the size and shape of an almond.

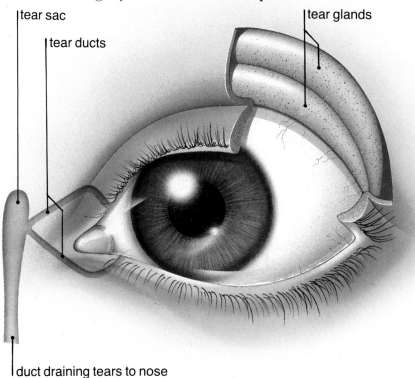

tear sac

tear ducts

tear glands

duct draining tears to nose

▷ The eye is kept moist and germ-free by tear fluid, which is produced continuously. The fluid drains away into the back of the nose and is eventually swallowed.

Fluid from the tear gland drains down the eye and collects in the inner parts of the eyelids. Here, there are two tiny holes – the entrances to the tear ducts. If you gently pull the lower eyelid outward, you can see the lower hole. Besides washing the eye, tear fluid contains a natural chemical called **lysozyme**. This acts as a disinfectant, helping to kill any germs on the eye and prevent infection.

Each blink sweeps used tear fluid from the surface of the eye into the tear duct. It also squeezes fluid already in the duct downward to where it opens into the tear sac, which eventually opens into the back of the nose.

◁ People from some mountainous parts of Eastern Asia, such as this girl from China, have an extra fold of skin in the eyelid which protects the eye from strong light. The Inuit people also have this extra fold of skin, to protect their eyes from the bright light that is reflected off the snow.

Defects of vision

Some common eye defects are due to faults in the growth of the eye, making it too short or too long.

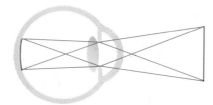

△ In a normal eye, a sharp image is formed on the retina.

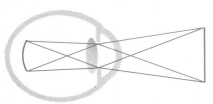

△ In **myopia**, the image is formed in front of the retina.

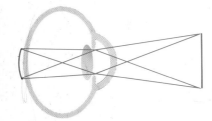

△ In **hypermetropia**, an image is produced behind the retina.

Like other parts of the body, the eyes vary in size from person to person. The size and shape of the eye influence its ability to work well and focus light correctly. In some people, the cornea or the lens is not quite the right shape, or the eyeball is too big or too small. This is rarely due to disease or illness. Usually it is simply a result of the way the body grows. But it does cause difficulties in seeing, which are called defects of vision.

One main defect is nearsightedness, or **myopia**. The eyeball is too big for the focusing power of the cornea. Either the eyeball is too long from front to back, or the cornea is too rounded. Nearby objects are seen clearly. But the lens cannot flatten enough to bring light rays from a distant object into focus on the retina. Instead they are focused in front of the retina, so the image of a distant object is blurred.

Another defect is farsightedness, or **hyper-metropia**. Here, the eyeball is too small for the focusing power of the lens. Either the eyeball is too short from front to back, or the lens is too flat. Faraway things are seen clearly, but the lens cannot bulge enough to bend rays of light from a near object so that they focus on the retina. Instead, they are focused behind it and, as a result, the image of a nearby object is blurred.

A third defect is **astigmatism**. The combined curvatures of the cornea, lens and retina do not match each other, so the image is distorted. It is as though, when looking at graph paper, the horizontal lines can be seen sharply, yet the vertical ones are blurred – or the other way round. A person may have astigmatism as well as being nearsighted or farsighted.

As we grow older, the lens may lose its suppleness and elasticity. It tends to stay in its distance-focusing slim shape and is less able to bulge. This is called **presbyopia** and is why some older people have difficulty reading or sewing.

As a defect of vision develops, we may be able to cope at first by trying extra-hard to focus on things. But this can put a strain on the muscles around the eye, eyelids, face and neck. This can lead to headaches, one early sign of a visual defect.

▽ Eye defects may be remedied with eyeglasses or contact lenses. Eye-tests are painless and should be done at least every two years. Here, the optometrist is looking into a patient's eye for early signs of disease or damage.

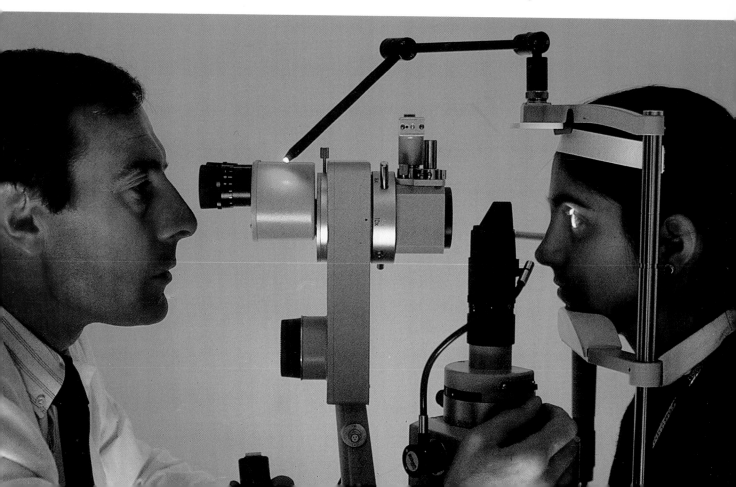

Eyeglasses and contact lenses

In the past, people with visual defects were at a definite disadvantage. In most countries today, however, people can wear eyeglasses or **contact lenses** to correct their eyesight. Today, eyeglasses (or "glasses") are not all made of glass – the lenses may be made of a special hard, clear plastic. This has advantages. If something hits a plastic lens, it may crack, but it will not shower the eye with tiny glass splinters. Also, plastic is lighter than glass, so it is more comfortable for those who wear thick lenses. In other respects though, glass lenses are better than plastic ones. Glass is harder and more resistant to scratches and the eventual "hazing" which occurs with wear and tear.

Each of the main types of visual defect can be helped by eyeglass lenses of a certain shape.
A concave lens is used for correcting myopia. This lens is thinner in the center than around the edges (although the whole lens is curved to match the surface of the eye). It bends the light rays outward before they reach the eye, so the rays will focus on the retina instead of in front of it.

Farsightedness requires convex lenses. These are thicker in the middle than around the edges. They bend the light rays inward so they focus on the retina instead of behind it.

Astigmatism is corrected by a lens that is more spoon-shaped, so it alters horizontal and vertical parts of the scene by different amounts. The result is an evenly focused image on the retina. This may be combined with myopia or farsightedness.

△ Some older people develop a form of farsight, as the lens ages and is less able to bulge for near vision. One sign of this is holding a newspaper at arm's length in order to bring the small print into focus. But the words may then be almost too far away to see clearly. Eyeglasses can help this problem.

34

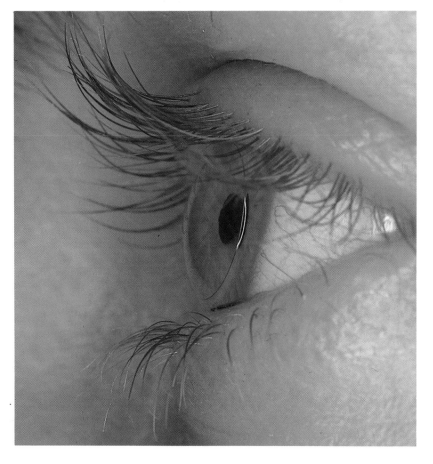

◁ Contact lenses can be used to correct far or near-sight. They are inserted by pulling back the eyelid and placing the lens directly on the cornea.

In some people, especially the elderly, the lens in the eye loses its elasticity so it cannot alter its shape easily. One answer is to wear **bifocal** eyeglasses. These look like ordinary glasses but have lenses of a different curvature set into the lower parts of the main lenses. When one looks ahead, which usually means at a distant object, the main lenses correct vision by the necessary amount. When one looks down, the thicker inset lenses give the extra correction needed to see near objects sharply, when reading a book for instance.

Contact lenses are shaped like eyeglass lenses and work in the same way, but they are much smaller. They are called contacts because they fit on the front of the eye, in contact with it.

Contact lenses

The first contact lenses were fitted as long ago as 1887 by a Swiss physician. They were made of glass and were very heavy and uncomfortable. Now, three main types of lens are available.

● **Hard lenses** cover only the central area of the cornea and are very efficient at correcting vision.

● **Soft lenses** cover the whole cornea. They are 30-75 percent water and so are more flexible. This makes them more comfortable. However, their flexibility means that they do not correct some eye problems as accurately as hard lenses.

● **Gas permeable lenses** are similar to hard lenses, but they are porous, allowing air to reach the surface of the eye. This means that they can be worn for longer periods.

Protecting your eyes

Diseases of the eye

- **Conjunctivitis** Inflammation of the **conjunctiva** (the membrane covering the eye), caused by a virus or bacteria (a germ), allergy or injury. It is only contagious if it is caused by a germ.
- **Trachoma** Inflammation of the inner surfaces of the eyelids. It is one of the most common causes of blindness in Africa and Asia. Trachoma is caused by bacteria and is very contagious.
- **Night blindness** Deficiency of Vitamin A leads to a loss of visual purple and makes it difficult or impossible to see in dark or dim conditions.
- **Stye** Infection of an eyelash follicle—the tiny pit, or hole, in the skin from which the eyelash grows.

The eyes are able to care for and protect themselves in many ways. Some of these, like blinking, happen automatically. We can help by taking precautions and by getting expert advice and treatment if something should go wrong.

One of the most obvious ways we can help is to protect the eyes from injury. In most countries it is a legal requirement to wear a helmet and visor or goggles during work that could endanger the eyes. This is especially true for people working with grinding machines, chemicals that may splash, and flying sparks. We should also take care of our eyes in potentially dangerous situations at home and in the garden.

Physical damage is not the only risk. Ultra-bright lights can harm the eyes, which is why welders wear specially darkened visors. You should never look directly at the sun; it will damage your eyes. Fumes and smoke can also be a threat to the health of the eyes. When your eyes become red and watery in a smoky place, it is nature's way of telling you that you need to get away from the hazard.

Headaches and eyestrain can also be problems. They may be caused by a defect of vision, which eyeglasses or contact lenses could correct. Or they could be due to too much close, detailed work, or working in a poor light. People who use computer monitor screens for long hours or watch a bright television set in dark surroundings, may also suffer from headaches.

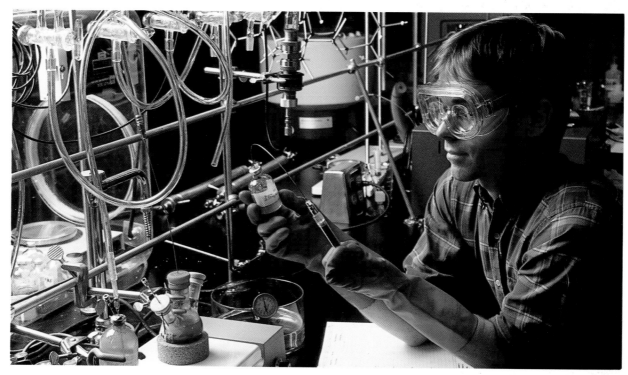

These are all good reasons to visit an optometrist at least every two years. The optometrist gives an eye examination, a vision test and general advice. The test will detect a visual defect, and glasses or contact lenses can be prescribed. Wearing these can only help – they do not encourage the eyes to get worse. The optometrist also examines the eyes and checks their general health. Certain signs inside the eye may point to eye diseases such as **glaucoma** (see page 22) or reveal health problems elsewhere in the body.

You should consult a doctor at once if you have pain in the eye or if your vision goes hazy, or wobbly, or dark, or changes in some other way. If a chemical splashes into your eyes, wash it out immediately with plenty of clean, cool water, and visit a hospital casualty department at once. And do not use eye drops or ointments unless they are advised by a doctor or an optometrist.

△ In dangerous activities, such as work in a chemical laboratory, it is important to make sure that the eyes are protected by safety glasses or goggles.

Color blindness

True color blindness (**monochromatic vision**) is the inability to distinguish color. The eye sees only black, white and shades of gray, like an old black and white movie. This condition is very rare. More common are other forms of color deficiency, such as not being able to tell the difference between red and green clearly (**anomalopia**).

Detecting color is a very complex process. It depends on the three types of light-sensitive cells in the retina. It also depends on the brain interpreting information from the eye correctly. It even depends on how well the colors and their names are learned during childhood. If one part of the process goes wrong, color deficiency may result.

In general, across Europe and North America, about one male in twelve has some form of color blindness. However, it affects only one female in two hundred. This is because color blindness is linked to the genes that turn a developing baby into a boy rather than a girl. For the same reason of inheritance, color blindness tends to run in families.

Color blindness is usually much less serious than it sounds. A color blind person can often guess the color of something from its shade. Shapes and positions of objects also give clues to their color, as with traffic lights. However, being color blind may mean that you cannot do certain jobs, such as being an airline pilot, a photographer or a fashion designer! It may also cause problems when playing computer games!

Color blindness is detected by showing a person special pictures made of colored dots. Certain colors make a pattern, such as a number. With a color deficiency, the person sees another pattern.

▽ With normal vision you see the number 29. If you have a red-green defect, you see the number 70.

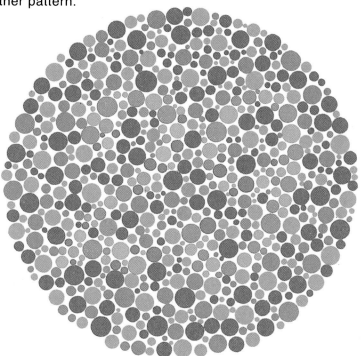

▽ If you read number 15, your color vision is normal. If you see 17, you may have a red-green defect.

▽ If you can see the number 45, you have normal vision. Most people with a color defect cannot see any number.

▽ Number 73 is seen by those with normal vision. No number is apparent if vision is defective.

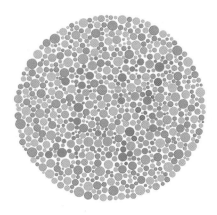

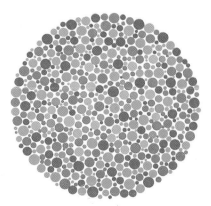

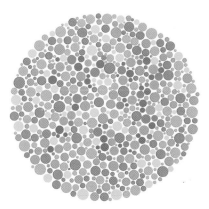

The mind's eye

Tricking the eye

When we watch a movie, we do not see that it is made up of many still pictures. Most television and cinema "moving pictures" are in fact made of still pictures shown very quickly, one after the other, at the rate of about 16 to 25 pictures each second. The still pictures follow each other so rapidly that the eye is still registering the last one when the next one is shown. So the pictures *blur* into one another, and in our minds we see them as one continuous, moving scene.

Animals whose eyes react faster than ours do not experience this blurring. So when a cat, for example, looks at a television screen it sees a series of still pictures, each one separate and unmoving, flicking past before its eyes.

The retina in the eye detects an image and partly processes it. Then the information is fed to the brain in the form of coded electrical signals. From these, the brain interprets what the eye sees and conjures up a moving picture in its "mind's eye." This is not a real image, like the image a movie projector shines on a screen. It is in the form of tiny electrical impulses.

The picture is not exact. The brain has many other jobs to do and these affect how we make sense of what we see. The picture is particularly affected by memory and experience. When we are babies, we have to learn to see. We learn certain rules; we learn that when a given object is big in our field of

▷ In this picture the church is a small model, yet looks the same size as the church in the other picture. The brain checks to see if it is in front or behind the children, giving the clue to its real size and position.

vision, it is nearby, and when it is small, it is far away. After a time, the brain begins to "jump to conclusions" about many things so that we do not have to interpret every scene afresh. If a person is large in our field of vision, we assume that the person is of normal size and nearby – not a giant some distance away.

The picture is also affected by other senses, such as smell. We may remember the fragrance of a rose. Then, later on, the same smell may bring back "memory pictures" and we can see the rose in our mind. Mood and tiredness also affect what we see, or rather, what we think we see. We may even "see" vivid pictures in our dreams, with eyes closed.

The brain can be tricked by "puzzle pictures." It tries to make sense of them, and sometimes fools itself in the process. Often the pictures are two-dimensional drawings, on paper, of something that would be impossible to make as a three-dimensional object.

△ The eye interprets what it sees by comparing it with previous memories. An "impossible" picture, like this staircase, is disturbing because it does not fit in with our previous experience.

◁ We know the church is in the distance, because it is so much smaller than the children.

Mixing colors

Colors of the spectrum

The colors of light we see are part of a much wider spectrum. At one end of the spectrum are ultra-violet rays, X-rays and gamma rays, and at the other end lie infrared rays, microwaves and radio waves. We can see none of these rays.

The primary colors of the spectrum, red, green and blue, combine to give white light.

Not all animals see in color. Humans do, and color is very important in our lives. In prehistoric times, early humans could tell by the color of a berry or a piece of fruit whether it was ripe and good to eat or poisonous and to be avoided. Today we use colors in many things, from works of art to the color-coded lights on a control panel.

Seeing in color is very complex. It is thought that the ganglion cells, receiving electrical signals from the cones, compare the strengths of the signals from the three different types of cone. In one tiny area of the retina, strong signals from "red" cones, as compared to weak signals from "green" and "blue" cones, indicate to the brain that the color being seen is red.

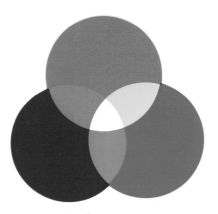

△ When blue, red and green lights are put together, white light is produced as they all overlap. These are the primary colors of light.

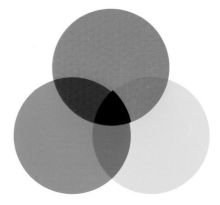

△ In printing or painting, all color can be produced from blue, red and yellow. Where the three overlap, black is produced. Blue, red and yellow are the three primary pigments in painting.

When the signals arrive in the brain, it is believed that they are separated into two groups. One group is concerned with the contrast between colors, while the other deals mainly with degrees of brightness.

Printers have "tricked" the eye for centuries. If you look at the colored pictures in this book through a magnifying glass, you will see they are made up of tiny dots. The dots come in three colors (the **primary pigments**) and black. The eyes and brain join these colors together to make patches of smooth color.

We also see colors in "opposite pairs." Red and green are one pair and blue and yellow are another. These are called **complementary colors**. Stare hard at a patch of one color, such as red, for half a minute. Then quickly look at a white area and you should see an **after-image** there in the complementary color of green.

▽ A close-up view of a color television screen shows that there are only three colors of dots – red, blue and green. From a normal viewing distance, the eye and brain join the colored dots together to make one smoothly-colored shape.

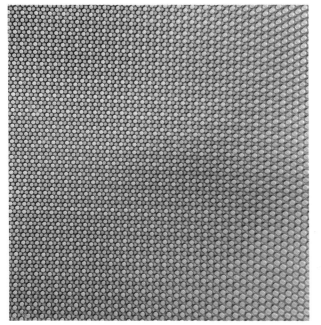

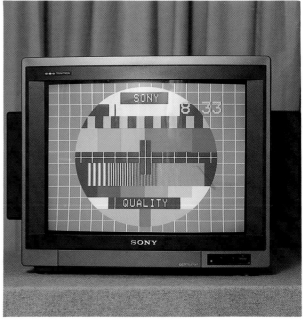

Vision and interpretation

Every day, with seemingly no effort, we look at our surroundings and make sense of what we see. Colors, brightness, shapes, shadows, movements, perspective and parallax are just some of the clues detected by the eyes and interpreted by the brain. But what we think we see is not always what is actually there.

We recognize the color of an orange from experience. We expect an object that is shaped like an orange, and feels and smells like one, to be orange in color. In a dim room, or in bright sunshine, we see its color as "orange." Yet scientific measurements of color photographs show that the true color of the orange varies enormously under these conditions. We can be tricked about the color of objects, such as cars, that come in different colors. Under bright yellow sodium street lights, an unfamiliar car may look gray. Yet in daylight it looks green. This is because we have no prior experience of the color that particular car may be.

Learning and language also have an effect on the colors we "see" in the brain. If a language does not have a word for a certain color, it may be grouped with another similar color and called by the same name.

Experience and learning also affect the way we interpret patterns. People have been shown several simple pictures made up of just a few dots or lines. They try to remember them and draw them later. If the pictures represent familiar objects, such as a face or a house, they can do the test well.

△ The human brain always tries to find a meaning in every image it sees. This image may be interpreted as an old lady with an outstretched hand, or as the man in the moon.

44

But with more random and "meaningless" patterns, people find the test much harder. In addition, it is known that the patterns and shapes which occur regularly in our surroundings depend to some extent on where we are brought up.

"Puzzle pictures" work because, in trying to make sense of what it sees, the brain comes up with two or more options. Often it cannot decide between them and it "switches" from one to the other. Such pictures are usually artificial. If these images appeared regularly in the real world, the brain would learn how to make sense of them.

By recognizing the familiar, and imposing meaning on it, the brain is able to notice significant things in its view of the world. It can quickly process the multitude of visual information from the eyes and interpret anything important. Finally, our sense of vision is combined with information from our other senses – sounds, smells, tastes and so on – to give us an all-round picture of the world about us.

Glossary

Accommodation: ability of the eye to adjust the shape of its lens in order to focus clearly on both near and distant objects.

After-image: looking at an object, then looking away and still seeing its "ghost-like" image, in a complementary color.

Anomalopia: a form of color blindness in which reds and greens look much the same.

Aqueous humor: thin, transparent liquid filling the forward part of the eye.

Astigmatism: visual defect resulting from a fault in the curvature of the cornea.

Bifocals: glasses designed with two sections on each of the lenses, so that a person with faulty accommodation can view both near and distant objects.

Bipolar cells: retinal cells, each with two long "tails," that receive nerve signals from rods and cones and pass them on to ganglion cells

Blind spot: area where nerve fibers and blood vessels leave the retina. It does not contain light-sensitive cells, and is therefore "blind."

Blink reflex: automatic closing of the eyelids, which protects (when something comes near the eyes) and cleans (when dust falls on to their surfaces) as well as spreading tear fluid over their surfaces to keep them moist.

Cataract: visual defect caused by clouding of the lens.

Choroid: layer between the retina and sclera which supplies blood to the eye.

Ciliary muscles: ring of very small muscles that change the shape of the lens to allow focusing.

Color blindness: visual defect in which recognition of certain colors is distorted. There are many different types of color blindness; red–green blindness is the most common.

Complementary colors: color "opposites." After-images are usually of a color that is complementary to the color being viewed.

Cones: light receptor cells with pointed ends. Cones register color and bright light, and are important in viewing fine detail.

Conjunctiva: very thin, transparent and sensitive covering of the front of the eye, that folds back to line the insides of the eyelids.

Contact lens: small, specially-shaped lens to correct a visual problem like nearsightedness, that sits on the front of the eye (in "contact" with the eye).

Convergence: tendency of the two eyes to point slightly inward as they view the object. Convergence becomes more marked as the object viewed moves closer to the eyes.

Cornea: transparent covering of the front of the eyeball.

Cortex: part of the brain's surface where information received is sorted and acted upon.

Field of vision: the area that can be seen without moving the eyes.

Fovea: small area on the retina in which cone cells are thickly clustered. The eye moves so that the center of the image we see is focused on the fovea.

Ganglion cells: nerve cells in the retina that transfer messages from the rods and cones to nerve fibers which pass to the brain.

Glaucoma: eye condition in which the pressure of fluid inside the eye builds up and causes pain and visual problems.

Hypermetropia: far or long-sightedness. Visual defect in which the eye cannot focus clearly on near objects.

Iris: ring-shaped muscular screen at the front of the eye, which opens and shuts to regulate the amount of light reaching the lens. The iris is usually colored blue or brown.

Lachrymal gland: almond-shaped gland just above the eye (in the orbit) that makes tear fluid.

Lens: rounded, transparent structure which focuses images onto the retina. The lens of the eye differs from glass lenses in being flexible. It is therefore able to focus the image of objects which are near or far.

Lysozyme: a natural disinfecting agent that is produced in tears. It kills micro-organisms that could otherwise grow on the cornea.

Melanin: dark pigment made by special cells in the body (melanocytes).

Monochromatic vision: seeing only in black, white and shades of gray (a rare form of color blindness).

Myopia: near- or short-sightedness. Visual defect in which the eye cannot focus clearly on far objects.

Night blindness: loss of visual purple due to deficiency of Vitamin A, which makes it difficult for the person to see in dark or dim conditions.

Optic chiasma: point at which the two optic nerves join and the nerve fibers from the central halves of the retinas cross to the opposite sides of the brain.

Optic nerve: bundle of nerve fibers that carry signals from each eye to the brain.

Orbit: cone-shaped hole or "socket" in the skull bone which houses the eye.

Parallax: when near objects seem to cross over distant ones as you move your head from side to side.

Peripheral vision: the ability to perceive objects while we are not looking directly at them. Peripheral vision uses rod cells at the edges of the visual field, and is therefore less sensitive than normal vision, where light falls on the fovea.

Perspective: when things look smaller and closer together the farther away they are, e.g. when railway lines look as though they come together and join in the distance.

Photoreceptors: rods and cones, the light-sensitive cells of the retina.

Presbyopia: loss of elasticity in the lens with age, so that it cannot bulge to focus on nearby objects.

Primary pigment: one of the three colors red, blue and yellow, mixed to create all other colors in printing.

Pupil: small hole in the middle of the iris. It opens and closes to keep the proper amount of light entering the eye.

Retina: inner lining of the rear part of the eye, in which the rod and cone cells are located.

Rhodopsin: purple pigment contained in rod cells, which is bleached by light, causing the cell to produce an electrical signal. Also called "visual purple."

Rods: thin, cylindrical cells in the retina, which respond to light, but cannot distinguish colors. They are very sensitive, and provide vision in areas with poor lighting.

Sclera: the creamy-white covering of most of the eyeball. It is thick and tough, giving the eye its rounded shape.

Stereoscopic vision: ability to detect depth in what we see, due to interpretation of slightly different pictures received from each eye. Also called binocular vision.

Strabismus: "squint" or "wandering eye," when a person's two eyes do not look at the same object.

Tear fluid: watery liquid which washes over the conjunctiva and cornea when you blink.

Trachoma: chronic contagious disease which if left untreated, commonly results in blindness.

Visual cortex: region at back of brain that receives and interprets nerve messages from the eyes.

Vitreous humor: clear, jelly-like material filling the eyeball, behind the lens. Light passes freely through the vitreous humor.

Yellow spot: another name for the fovea.

Index

PRINTED IN BELGIUM BY
proost
INTERNATIONAL BOOK PRODUCTION